Sam and Pat

Beginning Reading and Writing

Gan Noe

BOOK TWO

Jo Anne Hartel • Betsy Lowry • Whit Hendon

HEINLE
CENGAGE Learning

Australia • Brazil • Japan • Korea • Mexico • Singapore • Spain • United Kingdom • United States

HEINLE
CENGAGE Learning™

Sam and Pat 2: Beginning Reading and Writing
Jo Anne Hartel, Betsy Lowry, Whit Hendon

Publisher, Adult and Academic: *James W. Brown*

Senior Acquisitions Editor, Adult and Academic: *Sherrise Roehr*

Director of Product Development: *Anita Raducanu*

Editorial Assistant: *Katherine Reilly*

Director of Product Marketing: *Amy Mabley*

Senior Field Marketing Manager: *Donna Lee Kennedy*

Product Marketing Manager: *Laura Needham*

Production Editor: *Erika W. Hokanson*

Print Buyer: *Mary Beth Hennebury*

Development Editor: *Julie Cormier*

Compositor: *Cadmus Communications*

Project Manager: *Andrea Clemente*

Illustrators: *Megan Purdum, Michael Roehr*

Cover Designer: *Lori Stuart*

Library of Congress Number: 2005930727

ISBN-13: 978-1-4130-1965-0

ISBN-10: 1-4130-1965-X

International Student Edition: 1-4130-1971-4

Heinle
25 Thomson Place
Boston, MA 02210
USA

Cengage Learning is a leading provider of customized learning solutions with office locations around the globe, including Singapore, the United Kingdom, Australia, Mexico, Brazil and Japan. Locate our local office at:
international.cengage.com/region

Cengage Learning products are represented in Canada by Nelson Education, Ltd.

Visit Heinle online at **elt.heinle.com**
Visit our corporate website at **cengage.com**

Printed in the United States of America
3 4 5 6 7 8 9 10   11 10 09

Contents

Acknowledgments iv
Introduction v
Teaching Suggestions vii
Sample Lesson xi
Lesson Chart xii
Who are Sam and Pat? xiv

Lesson 1 Sunday Dinner 2
Lesson 2 Sam Gets a Raise 10
Lesson 3 Money, Money, Money! 14
Lesson 4 Problems in the House 18
Lesson 5 Buddy Is a Teen 22
Lesson 6 A Problem at School 31
Lesson 7 School and Buddy 36
Lesson 8 Sam's Dad 44
Lesson 9 Sam's Family in the Morning 49
Lesson 10 Here Comes Granddad 53
Lesson 11 Granddad and Buddy: Part 1 60
Lesson 12 Granddad and Buddy: Part 2 67
Lesson 13 Pat Is Sick 72
Lesson 14 Pat Makes an Appointment 77
Lesson 15 Pat Goes to the Doctor 82
Lesson 16 The Baby 87
Lesson 17 A Baby Has to Have a Lot of Things 90
Lesson 18 We Have No Crib 96
Lesson 19 Not a Good Spot 100
Lesson 20 The Ticket 104
Lesson 21 The Contest 112
Lesson 22 Second Best 116
Lesson 23 It's a Girl! 121
Lesson 24 The Baby Is Well 125

Phonetic Word Grids 129
Key Word Cards for Phonics 141
Suggested Listening Scripts 144

Acknowledgments

The inspiration for *Sam and Pat* came originally from Sylvia Greene, whose basal reader, *Sam and Val*, is the model for our work. In fact, we would never have conceived of *Sam and Pat* without Sylvia's encouragement and permission to use her ideas and her main character, Sam.

We would especially like to acknowledge Joann Wheeler, the talented artist who did the original drawings for this work. With deftness and simplicity, she breathed life into the characters and helped to make the stories more real for the readers.

This work would not have been possible without the funding and ongoing support of the Massachusetts Department of Education and everyone involved in the YALD Project. Special thanks go to Ashley Hager, Allyne Pecevich, Sheila Petruccelli, and Betty Stone, who helped us produce the first version of the book. Many thanks to Bob Bickerton and Jackie Fletcher as well as for their continual support throughout the project.

We would also like to thank those people who provided us with essential knowledge about the reading process. Like many other English language teachers working in adult basic education, we are always trying to come up with good materials and techniques for teaching English language learners at the beginning literacy levels. The YALD Theory and Practice in Reading Course, designed for teachers in the Boston area by John Strucker, gave us much needed background in teaching reading and exposure to a variety of teaching materials and methods. In addition, we would also like to thank Barbara Wilson for her Wilson Reading System, which informed our writing of the stories and our teaching.

Thanks to our colleagues at the Community Learning Center, who helped us all along the way and contributed ideas to this project. Special thanks to Ann Haffner for her suggestions, expertise, and ideas for organizing the book, and to John Galli, whose early contributions and enthusiasm kept us moving. Our gratitude goes to Mina Reddy, who helped us find time in our schedules to write the stories. Thanks also to proofreaders, Deb Foxx and Linda Huntington.

And last but certainly not least, we would also like to thank our students at the Community Learning Center, whose determination to learn to speak, read, and write English was the motivation for *Sam and Pat*. Their reactions to the stories and exercises as well as their contributions to the storyline were invaluable.

References

Kaufman, Lorna M., Ph.D., and Pamela E. Hooks, Ph.D. "The Dyslexia Puzzle, Putting the Pieces Together." New England Branch of the Orton Dyslexia Society, 1996.

Rosewell, Florence G. and Jeanne S. Chall. *Reading Difficulties, Effective Methods for Successful Teaching.* Elizabethtown, PA.: Continental Press, 1999.

Rosewell, Florence G. and Jeanne S. Chall. *Creating Successful Readers, A Practical Guide to Testing and Teaching at All Levels.* Itasca, IL.: The Riverside Publishing Company, 1994.

Schwarz, R. and L. Terrill. "ESL Instruction and Adults with Learning Disabilities." ERIC Digest. National Clearninghouse for ESL Literacy Education, Washington, DC. ED#EDO-LE-00-01 (June 2000).

Snow, C. and J. Strucker. "Lessons from preventing reading difficulties in young children for adult learning and literacy." *Annual Review for Adult Learning and Literacy* 1 (2000): 25-69.

Introduction

Sam and Pat is a basal reading series designed for English language learners who do not read or write in English. Some English language learners have little formal education and limited literacy skills in their native languages. Others come from countries that do not use the Roman alphabet, and still others have additional problems that could be the result of learning disabilities. All are struggling to learn English for the first time. Students at the most basic level are not yet comfortable holding a pencil and are slow or awkward when they are trying to write. *Sam and Pat* is intended to help beginning English language readers understand the alphabetic principle, that letter symbols represent sounds and that the sounds of the letters can be blended to make words. In addition, the stories in this book contain many words that the students are expected to learn as sight words. They are not to be learned by applying phonics but rather by remembering how they look.

Sam and Pat is a collection of stories, which follows a sequence of phonics skills. The actual phonics sequence appears in the lesson chart after this introduction. Each lesson starts with a picture or picture story that introduces the topic and new vocabulary. The stories are followed by comprehension and phonics exercises. The storyline of the book is loosely woven together since all the lessons are about family of the main characters, Sam and Pat.

Sam and Pat addresses some specific needs of English language learners:

1. The phonics sequence has been adjusted for English language learners who often have difficulty pronouncing and distinguishing certain sounds. For example, when an exercise requires the student to hear the difference between two sounds, the sounds first chosen are very different from each other. In a later lesson, one of the sounds is contrasted again with another that is more similar. The level of difficulty in exercises increases slowly.

2. Only simple words that students might encounter in their daily lives are used in the stories because literacy students have a limited vocabulary in English.

3. The stories are written with simplified grammar since long sentences and complex structures can interfere with comprehension.

4. Simplified themes from daily life have been incorporated into the stories because discussion of abstract ideas is not always possible when students' language skills are limited.

English Language Learners

English language learners sometimes have learning difficulties. These may be due to learning disabilities, a lack of exposure to English, unfamiliarity with the conventions of school, little or no facility with language learning, or a combination of these factors. Learning disabilities might be confused or obscured by issues connected with acquiring a new language. For example, a student might have trouble repeating back a sentence of more than three or four words because of phonological or auditory deficits. However, the problem may also be caused by limited educational background or lack of exposure to spoken English. English language learners bring different learning styles and abilities to the classroom. Some learn visually, while others need to interact with material by physically manipulating it. *Sam and*

Pat is meant for all beginning English readers and writers. The materials lend themselves to lessons that include listening, oral work, and hands-on activities, for example, with flash cards. Learners who have no learning disabilities will most likely be able to progress more quickly through the material than those who have learning disabilities.

The Lessons

Sam and Pat is designed for instruction in the following skills:

- Phonics
- Vocabulary
- Sight words
- Oral reading for accuracy
- Oral reading for fluency
- Silent reading
- Reading comprehension

Although the language in the stories is simple, some advance work is needed to clarify vocabulary and to introduce new concepts before the students actually read a lesson. *Sam and Pat* is only *one* component of an English language learner curriculum. Because the book focuses primarily on reading and writing, the material can be expanded with supplementary listening and speaking activities. The **Lesson Chart** lists the phonics skills and sight words covered in each lesson, as well as suggested vocabulary, grammar, and discussion topics.

Other Materials

In addition to the text, teachers may want to have other materials on hand, such as:

- The *Sam and Pat* audio program (available in CD or cassette format) for listening to the lesson stories
- A set of flash cards for key word pictures and letters for students to learn the sounds and names of the letters
- Sets of flash cards with sight words, one for each student to use
- Sets of letter cards for making words
- Cards with pictures on one side and corresponding words on the other for learning new words
- Separate picture and corresponding word cards for matching activities
- Sentences cut into words or phrases for students to put in order

Teaching Suggestions

Phonics for Reading

Phonics involves teaching the sounds of letters and then blending the sounds to make words. This skill is necessary for both reading and writing. Each lesson in *Sam and Pat* contains a target sound or sounds. Refer to the **Phonics** column in the Lesson Chart on pp. xii-xiii for the target sounds in each lesson.

Suggested Additional Materials

- **Key Word Cards for Phonics** See the pictures on pp. 141-143 for key words and sounds. These can be glued to 3 x 5 index cards and laminated. Every sound presented in the book should have a card (e.g., /e/, /th/, /ea/, /z/, etc.) Display the cards on the board tray or in a pocket chart. An ideal way to use these cards, if a magnetic board is available, is to attach magnetic tape to the backs of the cards so that they will stick to the board. For each card, say the name of the letter or letters, then the key word, and finally the sound. It is important to clip the pronunciation of the sounds; i.e., /p/ should remain voiceless and not pronounced "puh". /m/ is pronounced "mmm…" and not "muh." Review the names of the letters, key words, and their corresponding sounds for a few minutes in each class session.

- **Letter Cards** Make available to students sets of cards with individual letters. Make cards for consonants—b, c, d, f, g, h, j, k, l, m, n, n, p, qu, r, s, t, v, w, x, y, z, th, ch, sh, ck. Put vowels—a, e, i, o, u, ee, ea, ai, ay—on cards of a different color.

Suggested Activities

Select 10-12 phonetically regular words from your current lesson and previous lessons. Practice these words in a variety of ways.

- Write the words on flash cards or on the board. For each word, point to each letter and say the individual sounds. Then run your finger under the word as you say it to show students how to blend the sounds. Students repeat, then practice chorally and individually.
- Students can study their word cards independently or use them to quiz each other.
- Write the words on the board. Point to a word and ask for the letter that makes a certain sound. For example, in the word *mat:* What letter says /t/? What letter says /a/?
- Write the list of words on the board. Students read chorally and independently. Erase the first letter of a word, say the word, and students say the name of the letter that is missing. Proceed through the list, erasing initial consonants. Continue by erasing the last letters, and students again provide the names of the missing letters.
- Use letter cards for reading. Lay out letter cards to make words. Students read the words as a group and individually as you lay them out.
- Select a series of words that differ by one sound; e.g., *cat, cap, tap, top, mop,* etc. With the letters on the board tray, table, or magnetic board, ask students to read the words as you take out a letter and substitute a new one, progressing through the list.

Phonics for Spelling

Suggested Activities

- Use the **Key Word Cards for Phonics** on pp. 141-143 to reinforce the spelling of words in each lesson. Say the sound, and students respond with the name of the letter or letters that correspond to the sound.

- Have students use letter cards to form words. Dictate words with the target sound or sounds. If magnetic letters are available, students come to the board, and put words together as you dictate them. If individual sets of letter cards are used, students can do the same activity independently or in pairs.

- Select a series of words that differ by one sound (*cat, cap, tap, top, mop*). Students make words with the letter cards, substituting letters as you dictate new words.

Writing Exercises in *Sam and Pat*

Phonetic Word Grids

These grids, found on pp. 129-140, give students extra practice in identifying and writing phonetic words. Each grid corresponds to a lesson. Refer to the *Phonics* column in the **Lesson Chart** on pp. xii-xiii for the sequence of sounds. Review the pictures in the grid with students to make sure they understand the vocabulary and can interpret the pictures correctly. Read the list of words at the top of the page with students before assigning a grid.

"Listen and write the missing letters" activities

These activities are noted in the book by this icon: 🗩. You can use the **Suggested Listening Scripts** on pp. 144-145, or you can choose your own words. Choose phonetically regular words from the current lesson or previous lessons to dictate to students. The class repeats each word before filling in the missing sound. The sounds of the missing letters should be limited to ones that have already been taught.

"Listen and write" activities

These activities are also noted in the book by this icon: 🗩. You can use the **Suggested Listening Scripts** on pp. 144-145, or you can choose your own words. Again choose words from the lesson that contain the target sound. They can be the same words as in the "*Listen and write the missing letters*" activities. Students repeat the words before they write them. Students then read back the words that they have written.

"Circle the word you hear" activities

These activities are also noted in the book by this icon: 🗩. You can use the **Suggested Listening Scripts** on pp. 144-145, or you can choose your own words. Decide in advance which words students will circle, one word in each line. The class repeats the word you say before they circle it. At the end of the exercise, students read back the words that they circled.

Read/Write

Students read the list of words; e.g., in "Sam is Late to Work," *run, fun, gum, sun*, etc. Focus attention on the target sound /u/ by asking what letter is the same in all the words. Students repeat and then read the words as a group and individually. Ask for the number of the word you say. "What number is *sun?*" "What number is *hug?*" Ask students to read the list again in pairs or as a group.

Vocabulary and Sight Words

Some of the words in each lesson need to be recognized on sight. Some are new vocabulary words, and some are high frequency reading words. In both cases, they are not taught in the same manner as phonetically regular words because they are not phonetically regular (e.g., *the, are,* or *do*), or they have sounds not yet introduced. Sight words and vocabulary appear in the *New Sight Words* and *Suggested Vocabulary and Grammar Topics* sections in the **Lesson Chart** on pp. xii-xiii. Introduce these new words a few at a time and review old ones in every class session before reading a story.

Suggested Activities for Vocabulary

- Use pictures from the book, line drawings, photographs, and real objects. Students point to a picture, drawing, photograph, or real object as you say a word. Limit the number of words covered in each class session to no more than eight.
- Make flash cards with pictures and corresponding flash cards with words for students to match. As this set of cards grows, review.
- Play games with the flash cards. Give a definition or description of the word and have students pick out the correct flash card.
- Students sort cards according to topic; for example, days of the week, numbers, or family members.
- Play bingo with pictures and words.
- Give students a cloze exercise to fill in new vocabulary.
- Give students a worksheet with pictures to label.

Suggested Activities for Sight Words

- Present five to eight new sight words at a time.
- Review sight words from previous lessons.
- Write a sight word on the board in large letters. Say the word for students. Students repeat it. With an arm and index finger extended straight, demonstrate how to write the word in the air, while looking at the board and spelling the word out loud. Students do the same. Erase the word from the board, and students write it again in the air, spelling it aloud. Students pretend to write the word a third time with their finger on the table. Finally, they write it in their notebooks.
- Students keep a section in their notebooks for sight words.
- Using flash cards or the sight words written in their notebooks, students read, cover, spell aloud, and then write each word.
- Choose a combination of old and new sight words to dictate to students.

Reading and Reading Comprehension

Pre-reading

- Before reading a story, practice related grammar and content orally. Use the *Suggested Vocabulary and Grammar Topics* and the *Suggested Discussion Topics* from the **Lesson Chart** to plan listening and speaking activities that relate to the lesson. For example, before reading Lesson 9, "Sam Can't Get Up," review telling time, and teach daily routines and the present tense. Use dialogs, role-plays, and pictures for listening and speaking practice.

- Each lesson begins with an illustration or picture story. Discuss the picture or series of pictures with students, eliciting the story line and checking for comprehension of new words and topics. Students might label the pictures, copying words from the board. Help students to understand the story by relating it to their own experiences. After talking about an individual introductory illustration, ask the class to predict what will happen in the story.

Reading for Accuracy and Fluency

Students need many opportunities to practice so that they can read accurately and smoothly.

- Read the story aloud to the class and then have students read aloud. Individuals can take turns reading parts of the story.

- While students are reading the text, have them follow along by tracing under the words with the eraser end of a pencil or a finger.

- Encourage students to speed up and read more naturally by reading chunks of text consisting of two or three words at a time.

- Have pairs of students work together, reading to each other.

Reading Comprehension

A variety of activities and exercises help students develop comprehension skills.

- Cut up sequenced story illustrations. Give a set to individuals or pairs, who then put the pictures in the order of the story.

- Give students sentences from the story on strips of paper. They match pictures from the story to the sentence strips.

- Students put the sentence strips in the order of the story.

- Cut sentence strips in half and pass them out to individuals. Students match the sentence pieces by walking around the classroom and finding their partners.

- The class acts out dialogs or scenes from a story in pairs or small groups. Props, such as hats can help students get into character. Old telephones are useful in acting out situations such as phoning to make a doctor's appointment.

Sample Lesson

Book 1, Lesson 19: Sam Gets a Job

Objectives	Activities	Materials
1. **Conversation/Vocabulary/ Critical Thinking** Students discuss their skills and abilities at home and at work.	Make a chart with a column for students' names and another for actions: i.e., *sew, drive, speak English, cook, sing,* etc. Brainstorm abilities and match to individual students. Students make sentences about themselves using *can.* If there is time, students write some sentences about themselves.	Flash cards with pictures of actions and corresponding word cards
2. Students tell the story in Lesson 19 and learn new vocabulary: *bag, stock*	Students identify actions in the story, repeat sentences, and tell the story by looking at the pictures.	Introductory picture story in Lesson 19
3. **Phonics** Review the sounds /qu/, /r/, /j/, /g/, /w/, /ch/, /sh/, /ck/, /c/, /k/, short vowels	Use Key Word Cards for Phonics. Class works as a group. Students give the names of the letters, the key word, and then the sound of the letters.	Key Word Cards for Phonics
4. Review of words with short vowels and **st** blend: *can, boss, shop, mop, job, bag, well, think, hot, hat, hit, him, hum, hem, sock, stock, stick, sick*	Make words with letter cards. Students read the words by blending the sounds of the letters.	Flash cards with letters that can be strung together to form words
5. **Sight words** Students learn new sight words: *market, start, Monday, then, forgot, pay, maybe, talks*	Students "sky write," trace, copy words into their binders and on to their own packs of file cards for sight words.	Flash cards with sight words; file cards
6. **Oral Reading** Practice reading aloud, decoding.	The class reads the story aloud as a group and practices for fluency in pairs.	Copies of Lesson 19
7. **Reading Comprehension and Making Inferences**	Work on comprehension of the story orally. Ask: How does Sam feel? Do you think this is a good job for Sam? Why did he forget to ask how much the pay is?	Copies of comprehension questions for Lesson 19
8. **Writing/Phonics** Students review the spelling of the sounds: /qu/, /r/, /j/, /w/, /g/, /ch/, /sh/, /ck/, /c/, /k/, /b/, short vowels	"What says...?" Give the sound of a letter, and the students give the name of the letter.	Key Word Cards for Phonics
9. Students spell words with short vowel sounds and **st** blend.	Dictate a word, and students make words with letter cards: *stop, shop, mop, cop, Pat, pit, pot, not, nut, net, sick, stick*	Sets of letter cards for individuals or pairs of students to use
10. Students practice writing words with short **o** and **st**.	Students fill out worksheets.	Spelling exercises for Lesson 19

Lesson Chart

Lesson	Phonics	New Sight Words	Suggested Vocabulary and Grammar Topics	Suggested Discussion Topics
1 Sunday Dinner	• Vowels: diagraphs—**ee, ea** (Phonetic Word Grids 1 & 2)	Sunday, dinner, potatoes, ice cream, oven	• Food • Cooking verbs • **Will**	Food and nutrition
2 Sam Gets a Raise	• Vowels: digraphs—**ai, ay** (Phonetic Word Grids 3 & 4)	sunglasses, jacket, extra, sure, Tuesday, finish	• Robbery • Pay raise • Money	Crime
3 Money, Money, Money!	• Consonants: blends—**gr, fr, pr** (Phonetic Word Grid 5) • Vowel contrasts: **ea**/short **e** and **ai**/short **a**	money, excellent, good-bye, was, electricity, from	• How much? • Money	Money and bills
4 Problems in the House	• Vowels: review **ai, ea**	outside, drip, sofa, inside, ceiling	• Rooms • Furniture	• House problems • Furniture • Rooms
5 Buddy Is a Teen	• Consonants: blends—**cr, tr** • Vowels: review **ay, ee,** and short vowels	school, study, watch, drink	• **Like** • **Like to** • Numbers	• Relationships: parents and teens • Raising children
6 A Problem at School	• Consonants: blends—**gl, fl, pl** (Phonetic Word Grid 6) • Vowels: long **a** with silent **e** • Vowel contrast: long and short **a**	teacher, does, Ms.	• Negatives—present tense • Titles: **Dr., Ms., Mrs., Mr.,** etc.	• Children and school
7 School and Buddy	• Consonants: blends—**gr, br** (Phonetic Word Grid 7) • Vowels: long **a** with silent **e** (Phonetic Word Grid 8)	English	• School subjects • **When/what** questions	School in the U.S.
8 Sam's Dad	• Consonants: blends **bl** • Review—**gl, gr, tr, sl** • Vowels: long **i** with silent **e** (Phonetic Word Grid 9)	years, old, died, many, nobody, invite, smiles, o'clock, talk	Family	• Family • Taking care of elders
9 Sam's Family in the Morning	• Consonants: blends—**tw, sw** (Phonetic Word Grid 10) • Vowel review: **a** with silent **e** and **i** with silent **e**	morning, first, everybody, breakfast, family, next	• Time • Present tense • **Who** questions	Daily routines
10 Here Comes Granddad	• Consonants: blend review—**dr, cl, fl**; soft **c** • Vowel review: **a** with silent **e** and **i** with silent **e**	Granddad, always, never, lazy, some, away, that, think	• Adverbs: **always** and **never** • Present tense	Relationships: grandchildren and grandparents

Lesson	Phonics	New Sight Words	Suggested Vocabulary and Grammar Topics	Suggested Discussion Topics
11 Granddad and Buddy: Part 1	• Consonants: soft **c**, blend review—**gr** • Vowel review: **a** and **i** with silent **e**, short **a** and **i**	by, junk, food, out, room	Review: days of the week	Relationships: grandchildren and grandparents
12 Granddad and Buddy: Part 2	• Vowels: review short vowels **ay, ee**	Thursday, so	Present tense	• Negotiations • Problem solving • Relationships: grandchildren and grandparents
13 Pat Is Sick	• Consonants: blend review—**sl** • Vowels: **o** and silent **e** (Phonetic Word Grid 11)	night, calls, appointment, doctor	Calling the doctor	• Sickness • Appointments
14 Pat Makes an Appointment	• Consonants: blends—**sn, sc, sk** (Phonetic Word Grid 12) • Vowels: **i** and **o** with silent **e**	Dr., secretary	• Making an appointment • Sickness	• Sickness • Appointments
15 Pat Goes to the Doctor	Vowels: **u** and **o** with silent **e**, short **u** and **o**	pounds, clinic, having, baby, due	• Clinic • Doctor's office • Medical procedures/checkups	Medical topics
16 The Baby	• Consonants: review blends • Vowels: review silent **e**	boy, girl, day care, excited	• Future with **will** • Questions with **will**	• Hopes and dreams • Future plans
17 A Baby Has to Have a Lot of Things	**ing, ink, ong, onk, ang, ank, ung, unk**	beautiful, how, give	• Adjectives: describing things **(expensive, beautiful, big, pink)** • Colors	Shopping
18 We Have No Crib				
19 Not a Good Spot	Two syllable words with closed syllables	find, tomorrow	Quantifiers (**a gallon** of milk, a **dozen** eggs)	Cars
20 The Ticket				
21 The Contest	Review: two syllable words with closed syllables	Mr., first, hard, does, listen	• Present tense negative **(does not, do not)**	Music
22 Second Best			• Expressions of time **(every day, in six weeks)**	
23 It's a Girl!	• Conclusion and review: all two syllable, closed syllable words	girl, now	• **Have to/has to** • Present tense	Emergencies
24 The Baby Is Well	• review of **ll, ss, ff**			Babies

Who are Sam and Pat?

1. This is Sam. This is Pat. They are married.

2. Sam works at the Shop Well Market.

3. Pat works in a school. Her job is to fix lunch for the kids.

4. This is Buddy. He is the son. Buddy plays the trumpet.

5. Gus is a good friend. Gus has a taxi. He helps Sam.

6. They all have good days and bad days.

7. They are happy but they have problems. They have bills to pay.

8. Sam is late to work. Pat has the van. Sam wants the van.

9. Sam has a bad back.

10. What is next?

Lesson

1 Sunday Dinner

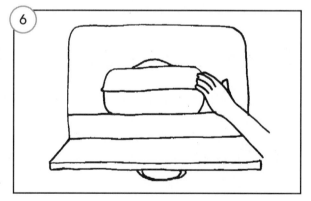

1. It is Sunday.

2. Sam, Pat, and Buddy have a big meal.

3. Dee is Buddy's friend.

4. Dee comes for dinner too.

5. Sam can clean and peel the beets.

6. Buddy can cut the green beans.

7. Pat can fix the meat and potatoes.

8. And last, they can eat peach ice cream.

9. It is 11:00. The meat is in the oven.

10. They hear POP! POP!

11. The oven has no heat.

12. Sam and Pat check the oven.

13. Sam can see the problem.

14. He can fix it.

15. Then the oven is OK.

16. They cook and eat.

17. Dee says, "Thanks! Thanks for a good meal!"

Write _Yes_ or _No_   **_Yes_ or _No_**

1. Dee is Buddy's sister.   1. _____

2. It is Monday.   2. _____

3. Sam can peel the meat.   3. _____

4. They can eat apple ice cream.   4. _____

5. The oven has no heat.   5. _____

6. Sam can fix the oven.   6. _____

7. They cook and eat.   7. _____

8. They have a good meal.   8. _____

Write the sentences next to the pictures.

Buddy can cut the green beans.

Sam can clean the beets.

Sam can fix the oven.

They can eat.

They hear POP! POP! The oven has no heat.

1. _____

_____

2. _____

_____

3. _____

_____

4. _____

_____

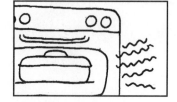
5. _____

_____

Circle the correct word. Write the word in the blank.

 1. He has no _____ .

heat
meat

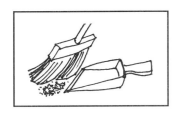 2. He can _____ the floor.

sheep
sweep

 3. He is at the _____ .

beach
peach

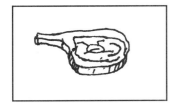 4. He likes to eat _____ .

heat
meat

 5. I have _____ children.

three
tree

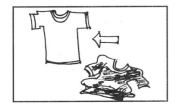 6. This shirt is _____ .

clean
lean

Circle the correct word. Write the word in the blank.

7. He can _____ .

lean
mean

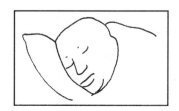

8. He can't _____ .

sheep
sleep

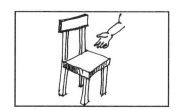

9. Please have a _____ .

neat
seat

10. Eat a _____ .

beach
peach

Read the words, cover the words, and write the words again.

1. meet _____

   beet _____

   feet _____

   street _____

2. see _____

   bee _____

   three _____

   Dee _____

3. sleep _____

   keep _____

   sweep _____

   sheep _____

Read the words, cover the words, and write the words again.

4. teach _____

   beach _____

   peach _____

5. clean _____

   bean _____

   lean _____

Sam Gets a Raise

 1. Sam is at work on Tuesday.

2. He is at work at the Shop Well Market.

3. Today he has to stay.

4. He can go home at 9:00 P.M.

5. At 5:00 a man comes in.

6. The man has sunglasses and a gray jacket.

7. The man speaks to Sam.

8. Man: Need extra cash?

   Sam: Sure!

   Man: Today you finish at 9:00.

         But wait for 9:30.

         Do not lock up.

         I will come and pay you $500 cash.

   Sam: OK!

9. But then Sam thinks, "This man will rob the market!"

10. "I will tell the boss. This man is no good."

11. At 9:30 the boss and Sam wait for the man.

12. They wait with the cops.

13. The cops grab the man.

14. The man will go to jail.

15. The boss is very happy.

16. Sam will get cash from the boss . . . $500.

Fill in the blanks with the correct words.

cash   go   sunglasses   rob

cops   pay   jail

1. Sam can _____ home at 9:00 P.M.

2. The man has a gray jacket and _____.

3. The man will _____ Sam $500.

4. Sam thinks the man will _____ the market.

5. The boss and Sam wait with the _____.

6. The man will go to _____.

7. Sam will get _____.

Read the words. Write.

1. raise   1. r____se

2. wait   2. w____t

3. chain   3. ch_____

4. jail   4. j_____

5. stay   5. st____

6. gray   6. gr____

7. pay   7. _____

8. day   8. _____

9. today   9. _____

10. Monday   10. _____

③ Money, Money, Money!

 1. Sam helps get the man with the gray jacket and sunglasses.

2. He gets $500 from the Shop Well Market.

3. $500 is very good. The money can help a lot.

4. The money can help pay the bills.

5. Gas and electricity cost a lot.

6. The last electricity bill was $55.

7. The rent cost $400.

8. The last telephone bill was $45.

9. Rent, electricity, and telephone . . .

10. How much is that?

11. $500! Good-bye!

Look at the story, and write the answers.

1. How much is Sam and Pat's rent? _____

   _____

2. How much is the electricity? _____

   _____

3. How much is the telephone bill? _____

   _____

4. How much are the 3 bills? $400
                                                 55
                                               45
                                       _____

5. What bills do you pay? _____

   _____

   _____

Circle the word for each picture.

 1. bead   bed

 2. teen   ten

 3. seat   set

 4. read   red

 5. mean   men

 6. main   man

 7. rain   ran

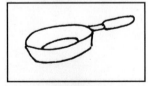 8. pain   pan

 9. pail   pal

Write the missing letters.

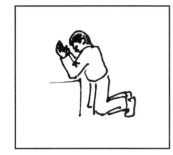 1. _ _ a y

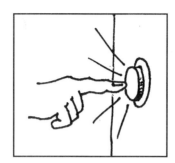 4. _ _ _ e s s

 2. _ _ o g

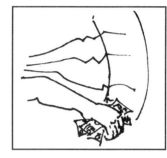 5. _ _ a b

 3. _ _ i n

Read the words.

1. frog
2. fresh
3. free
4. friend

5. grab
6. grass
7. grill
8. gray

9. grin
10. pray
11. press
12. print

Lesson

Problems in the House

 1. It is Saturday.

2. The house is clean.

3. Outside it is cold.

4. The rain will not stop.

5. Drip, drip, drip.

6. Sam is on the sofa.

7. His shoes are off.

8. Sam can hear drip, drip.

9. Drip, drip on the roof outside.

10. Drip, drip on Sam inside.

11. Sam can't rest.

12. He can see a big leak.

13. Sam and Pat have a big leak in the ceiling.

Write *Yes* or *No*.

1. Is it Saturday?   _____

2. Is the house clean?   _____

3. Is it hot outside?   _____

4. Is Sam in the kitchen?   _____

5. Is Sam on the sofa?   _____

6. Is the leak in the ceiling?   _____

Read the words.   **Write.**

1. rain   _____

2. nail   _____

3. pail   _____

4. jail   _____

5. pain   _____

6. mail   _____

Read the words.   Write.

1. clean   _____

2. leak   _____

3. eat   _____

4. ear   _____

5. peach   _____

6. heat   _____

Lesson

5 Buddy Is a Teen

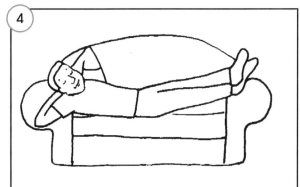

1. Pat is mad. Pat is sad. And Sam is mad.

2. Buddy is 15.

3. Buddy is a teen.

4. He is not happy at school.

5. He will not study.

6. He likes to sit on the sofa.

7. He likes to watch TV.

8. He likes to eat chips and drink pop.

9. He likes to play the trumpet.

10. And he will not help clean the house.

11. What can Sam and Pat do?

Write *Yes*, *No*, or *Maybe*.   ***Yes*, *No*, or *Maybe***

1. Buddy likes to study.   _____

2. Buddy likes to go to school.   _____

3. Buddy likes to clean the house.   _____

4. Buddy likes to watch TV.   _____

5. Buddy likes to play the trumpet.   _____

6. Buddy likes to eat chips.   _____

7. Buddy likes to drink pop.   _____

8. Buddy likes to cook.   _____

9. Buddy likes to work.   _____

10. Buddy likes to sleep.   _____

What do you like to do?

I like to _____

_____

_____

_____

_____

_____

_____

_____

Listen for *ai* or *ee*. Write *ai* or *ee* under the pictures.

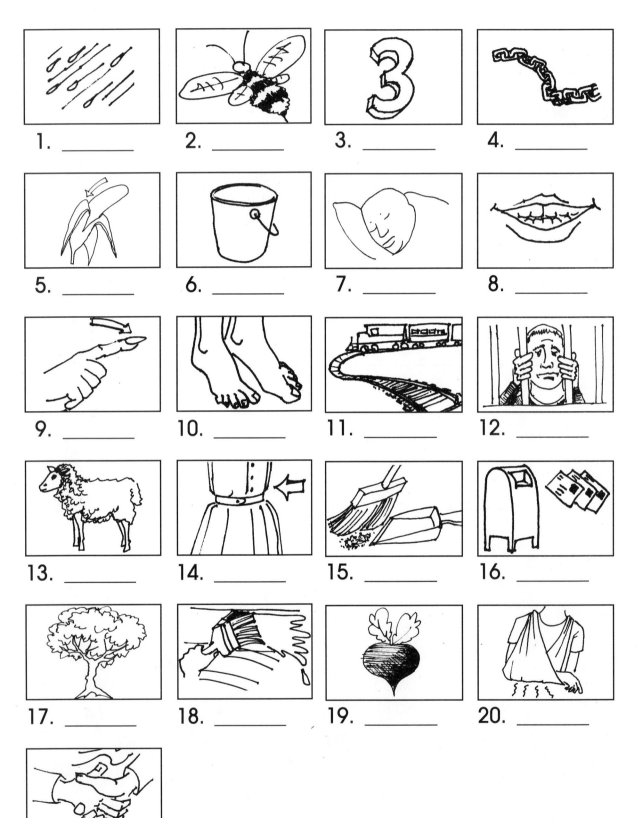

1. _____

2. _____

3. _____

4. _____

5. _____

6. _____

7. _____

8. _____

9. _____

10. _____

11. _____

12. _____

13. _____

14. _____

15. _____

16. _____

17. _____

18. _____

19. _____

20. _____

21. _____

Read the words.

1. teen
2. peel
3. sleep
4. feet
5. pay

6. day
7. say
8. may
9. gray
10. pray

Write.

1. _____

2. _____

3. _____

4. _____

5. _____

Add *teen*.   **Write the numbers again.**

1. 13 thir_____   13 _____

2. 14 four_____   14 _____

3. 15 fif_____   15 _____

4. 16 six_____   16 _____

5. 17 seven_____   17 _____

6. 18 eigh_____   18 _____

7. 19 nine_____   19 _____

Read the words.

1. tree
2. tray
3. trip
4. trash
5. truck

6. train
7. crab
8. crib
9. crack
10. crush

Write.

1. _____

2. _____

3. _____

4. _____

5. _____

Listen to the teacher. Look at the pictures.
Circle the words.

1. crab or cab
?

2. tuck or truck
?

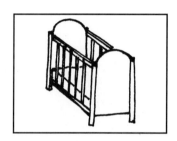

3. crib or rib
?

4. rack or crack
?

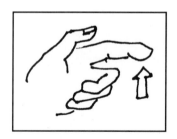

5. tip or trip
?

6. ray or tray
?

7. tree or tee
?

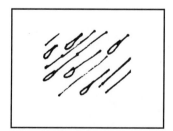

8. train or rain
?

Lesson

 6 **A Problem at School**

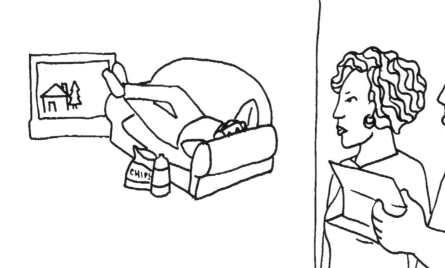

 1. Pat and Sam are not happy with Buddy.

2. Buddy hates school.

3. He does not study.

4. He gets to school late.

5. Pat and Sam meet with the teacher.

6. The teacher is Ms. Lane.

7. On Monday, Sam and Pat meet with Ms. Lane.

8. Maybe she can help.

9. Maybe Ms. Lane, Sam, and Pat can make a plan for Buddy.

Pat, Sam, Buddy, or _Ms. Lane?_

1. Who is not happy?   _____

2. Who hates school?   _____

3. Who needs help in school?   _____

4. Who gets to school late?   _____

5. Who will Sam and Pat see?   _____

Circle the correct word. Write the word in the blank.

1. This is a _____ .

can
cane

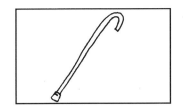

2. This is a _____ .

can
cane

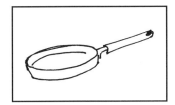

3. This is a _____ .

pan
pane

4. You can take a _____ .

plane
plan

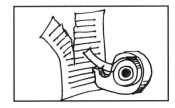

5. Fix this with the _____ .

tap
tape

6. This is a _____ .

mate
mat

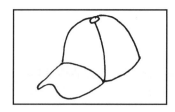

7. This man has a _____ .

cap
cape

8. This man has a _____ .

cap
cape

9. You can sit in the _____ .

shad
shade

Write the missing letters.

1. _ _ u g

4. _ _ a t e

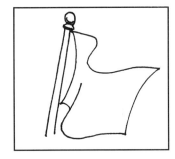
2. _ _ a g

5. _ _ a s s

3. _ _ a n t

Read the words.

1. glass

2. glad

3. flag

4. floss

5. flex

6. flip

7. plug

8. play

9. plate

10. plant

Lesson

7 School and Buddy

1. On Monday, Pat and Sam have to meet with the teacher.

2. Her name is Ms. Lane.

3. Buddy's grade in math is D.

4. D is not good.

5. English is the same.

6. Buddy has a D in English.

7. And he is late to school every day.

8. Ms. Lane can help Buddy.

9. She can help Buddy from 2:00 to 3:00 every Monday.

10. She can work on math and English with Buddy.

11. Then maybe Buddy can fix his bad grades.

Look at the story. Choose the correct answers.

When?

1. When does Ms. Lane meet with Sam and Pat?

   a. They meet on Thursday.

   b. They meet on Wednesday.

   c. They meet on Monday.

2. When can Ms. Lane help Buddy?

   a. She can help Buddy every day.

   b. She can help Buddy on Wednesday.

   c. She can help Buddy every Monday.

What?

3. What is Buddy's grade in math?

   a. Buddy's grade is B.

   b. Buddy's grade is A.

   c. Buddy's grade is D.

4. What is Buddy's grade in English?

   a. Buddy's grade is B.

   b. Buddy's grade is A.

   c. Buddy's grade is D.

5. What is the plan for Buddy?

   a. Pat and Sam can help Buddy.

   b. Buddy can get a job.

   c. Ms. Lane can help Buddy with math and English.

Fill in the blanks with the correct words.

grade	late	Lane
wake	hates	

1. D is Buddy's _____.

2. Ms. _____ is the teacher.

3. Buddy likes to sleep. He can't _____ up.

4. Buddy is not happy. He _____ school.

5. It's 9:30 A.M. Buddy is _____ to school.

Read.   **Write the missing letters.**

1. date   1. d__t__

2. late   2. l__t__

3. hate   3. h__t__

4. state   4. st__t__

5. wake   5. w__k__

6. make   6. m__k__

7. take   7. t__k__

8. cake   8. c__k__

Listen and write the words.

1. _____

2. _____

3. _____

4. _____

5. _____

6. _____

7. _____

8. _____

Write the missing letters.

1. __ __ a s s

4. __ __ a p e

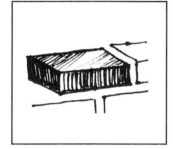

2. __ __ i c k

5. __ __ a d e

3. __ __ u s h

Read the words.

1. grab

2. grass

3. brick

4. bridge

5. grin

6. grill

7. grade

8. grape

9. braid

10. brush

8 Sam's Dad

 1. Sam has a dad.

2. His name is Mike.

3. Mike is 80 years old.

4. His wife died last year.

5. Mike is many miles from Sam and Pat.

6. Mike can't drive.

7. He can't cook.

8. He can't clean.

9. He has nobody to help him.

10. Pat says, "We can invite Mike to stay here."

11. Sam smiles. "My dad will like that."

12. Pat says, "Buddy will come home at five o'clock."

13. "We can talk to Buddy at five."

Fill in the blanks with the correct words.

Mike   cook   old   wife   stay   five

1. Sam's dad is _____.

2. Mike is 80 years _____.

3. Mike's _____ died.

4. Mike can't _____.

5. Buddy will come home at _____ o'clock.

6. Pat and Sam will invite Mike to _____.

Read the words.

1. black
2. bless
3. blade
4. blame

5. bleed
6. glad
7. glass

 Write.

1. _____
2. _____
3. _____
4. _____

5. _____
6. _____
7. _____

Fill in the blanks with the correct words.

lap   slip

1. Sit on my _____.

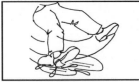

2. Don't _____.

back   black

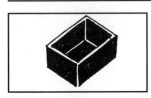

3. The box is _____.

4. This is his _____.

grass   gas

5. She sits on the _____.

6. The car needs _____.

rain   train

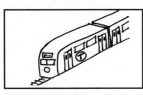

7. Get on the _____.

8. This is for the _____.

Sam's Family in the Morning

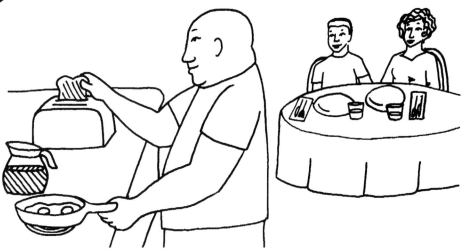

 1. This is Sam's family every morning.

2. Pat wakes up first. She gets up at 6:30.

3. Sam wakes up next. But he hates to get up.

4. Sam likes to stay in bed. He likes to sleep.

5. Pat makes Sam get up. "Wake up! It's time to get up!"

6. Pat wakes up Buddy too.

7. Sam makes breakfast for everybody.

8. Buddy rides his bike to school.

9. Pat drives the van to work.

10. Sam takes the bus.

11. But if it is late, Sam gets a ride in the van with Pat.

Sam, Pat, Mike, or Buddy?

1. Who wakes up first? _____

2. Who hates to get up? _____

3. Who wakes up Buddy? _____

4. Who makes breakfast? _____

5. Who rides his bike? _____

6. Who drives the van? _____

7. Who takes the bus? _____

Circle the correct word. Write the word in the blank.

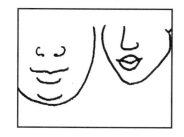

1. Pat and Sam _____ .

smell
smile
mile

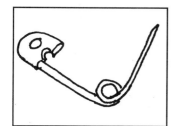

2. Can I have a _____ ?

pin
pine
spin

3. I can walk nine _____ .

mills
smiles
miles

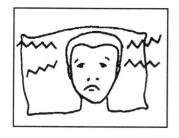

4. Buddy is _____ .

six
sick
kiss

5. He takes a big _____ .

bit
bite
bill

6. Here are _____ fish.

fine
fish
five

7. 10¢ is one _____ .

dime
dim
dish

8. Tea is a _____ .

drink
drip
drive

9. Pat is the _____ .

win
wife
wig

10. Eat some _____ .

ice
rice
mice

11. This is a fat _____ .

pig
pit
pine

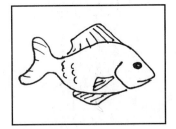

12. I like _____ .

five
fine
fish

Here Comes Granddad

1. Buddy is home at five.

2. Sam says, "We need to talk."

3. Sam says, "Granddad will come to stay here."

4. Buddy says, "Oh no! Not Granddad Mike!"

5. "Granddad is always mad."

6. "He never smiles."

7. "And Granddad has a pipe. I hate the pipe."

8. "And he always shakes his cane at me."

9. "And Granddad says I am lazy. I don't like that."

10. "I don't like my life," Buddy says.

11. Buddy runs outside.

12. He gets on his bike.

13. He rides away.

14. Pat says, "It is OK. Buddy needs some time to think."

Circle the letter of the correct answer.

1. Buddy is home at _____.

   a. 9:00

   b. 6:00

   c. 5:00

2. Granddad will stay with _____.

   a. his wife

   b. Pat, Sam, and Buddy

   c. Gus

3. Granddad shakes his _____.

   a. pipe

   b. hat

   c. cane

4. Buddy says Granddad Mike is always _____.

   a. mad

   b. happy

   c. nice

5. Granddad will come to stay. Buddy is _____.

   a. nice

   b. not happy

   c. happy

6. Buddy needs some time to _____.

   a. eat

   b. watch TV.

   c. think

Read.   **Write the missing letters.**

1. like   1. l__k__

2. bike   2. b_____

3. Mike   3. M_____

4. nine   4. n__n__

5. fine   5. f_____

6. pine   6. p_____

7. shine   7. sh_____

8. mine   8. _____

9. wine   9. _____

10. ice   10. i____

11. spice   11. sp_____

12. mice   12. _____

13. rice   13. _____

14. nice   14. _____

Circle the correct picture.

1. drive

2. drip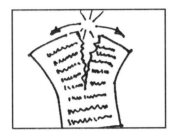

3. drink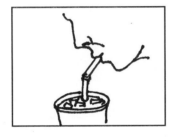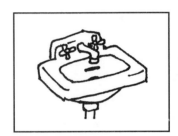

4. class

5. clock

 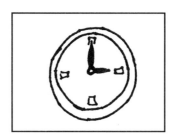

6. flip

 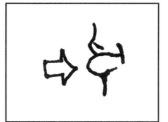

 Granddad and Buddy: Part 1

 1. On Friday, Granddad comes by plane.

2. Sam, Pat, and Buddy take Granddad home.

3. On Saturday, Granddad says, "Buddy, you eat too much junk food."

4. On Sunday, Granddad says, "Buddy, you can't play the trumpet in the house."

5. "Take the trumpet outside."

6. On Monday, Granddad says, "Buddy, you go out too much."

7. "And you always come home too late."

8. On Tuesday, Granddad says, "Buddy, this place is a mess!"

9. "It is time to clean your room."

10. Buddy thinks, "I need some space! Granddad, get off my back!"

Circle the letter of the correct answer.

1. Granddad comes by _____.

   a. plane

   b. train

   c. bus

2. Granddad hates _____.

   a. Buddy's hat

   b. Buddy's friend

   c. Buddy's trumpet

3. Buddy thinks Granddad is _____.

   a. happy

   b. sad

   c. a problem

Fill in the blanks with the correct words.

ice   rice   mice

1. They are _____.

2. I eat _____.

3. This drink has _____.

face   race   space

4. He has a nice _____.

5. Run in a _____.

6. I need _____.

Listen to the teacher and write the words again.

1. _____   4. _____

2. _____   5. _____

3. _____   6. _____

Circle the words you hear.

1. race   rice

2. space   spice

3. lake   like

4. bake   bike

5. make   Mike

Listen and write.

1. _____

2. _____

3. _____

4. _____

5. _____

Circle the correct words.

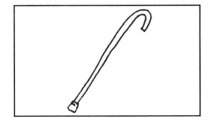

1. can   cane   2. plan   plane   3. hat   hate

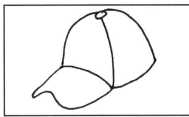
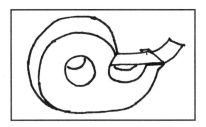

4. cap   cape   5. tap   tape

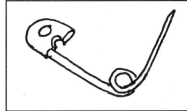

6. lick   like   7. pin   pine   8. dim   dime

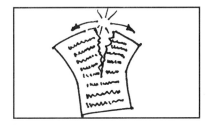

9. rip   ripe   10. sit   site

Listen to the teacher. Write *g* or *gr* under the pictures.

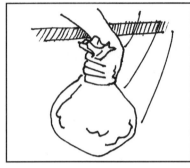

1. _____

2. _____

3. _____

4. _____

5. _____

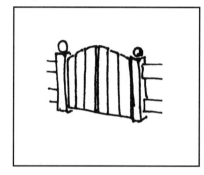

6. _____

7. _____

8. _____

9. _____

Granddad and Buddy: Part 2

 1. On Thursday, Buddy speaks to his mom and dad.

2. "I can't play the trumpet in the house."

3. "Granddad tells me to stop."

4. Buddy says, "I don't like my life here."

5. Sam says, "Buddy, wait. Your mom and I can talk to Granddad."

6. So Sam and Pat sit and talk with Granddad.

7. Pat says, "Granddad, you are not nice to Buddy."

8. Sam says, "Buddy is a good kid."

9. Granddad says, "Yes, Buddy is a good kid."

10. "But Buddy likes that trumpet. I hate it."

11. Granddad says, "Well OK, maybe I can talk to Buddy."

12. Granddad asks Buddy, "Do you like to play chess?"

13. Buddy says, "OK, a game of chess will be nice."

Circle the letters of the correct answers.

1. On Thursday Buddy speaks to _____.

    a. Sam and Pat

    b. Gus

    c. Dee

2. Granddad hates _____.

    a. Buddy's hat

    b. Buddy's friend

    c. Buddy's trumpet

3. Granddad thinks Buddy is _____.

    a. a bad kid

    b. a sad kid

    c. a good kid

4. Maybe Granddad and Buddy can _____

    a. play the trumpet

    b. go to bed late

    c. play chess

Read.   **Write the missing letters.**

1. sad   1. s__d

2. sit   2. s__t

3. pop   3. p__p

4. help   4. h__lp

5. study   5. st__dy

6. at   6. __t

7. chips   7. ch__ps

8. on   8. __n

9. rest   9. r__st

10. trumpet   10. tr__mpet

Read.   **Write the missing letters.**

1. teen   1. t____n

2. peel   2. p____l

3. sleep   3. sl____p

4. tree   4. tr____

5. feet   5. f____t

6. pay   6. p____

7. day   7. d____

8. say   8. _____

9. may   9. _____

10. play   10. _____

Lesson

13 Pat Is Sick

1. Pat does not feel good.

2. Every morning she feels sick.

3. Every night she is in bed at 9:30 P.M.

4. The smoke from Granddad's pipe makes her sick.

5. She can't cook fish.

6. The smell of fish on the stove makes her sick.

7. It is Friday morning. Pat has on her robe.

8. Pat says, "Sam . . . I am sick. I need to stay home."

9. "I can't go to work."

10. Pat picks up the telephone.

11. She calls the doctor.

12. She makes an appointment.

13. Sam says, "I hope the doctor can help."

Look at the story and answer the questions.

1. What is Pat's problem?

   _____

2. What makes Pat sick?

   _____

3. What does Pat say?

   _____

4. Who calls the doctor?

   _____

5. Who has an appointment?

   _____

Read.   **Write the missing letters.**

1. hope   1. h__p__

2. rose   2. r__s__

3. smoke   3. sm__k__

4. stove   4. st__v__

5. home   5. _____

6. note   6. _____

7. rose   7. _____

8. robe   8. _____

Listen to the teacher. Write _s_ or _sl_ under the pictures.

1. _____

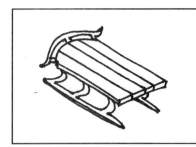

2. _____

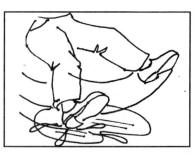

3. _____

4. _____

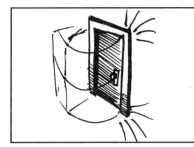

5. _____

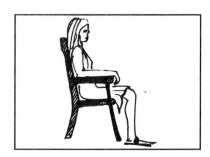

6. _____

7. _____

8. _____

9. _____

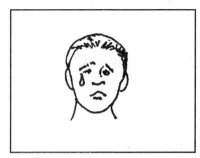

10. _____

14 Pat Makes an Appointment

Secretary:	Dr. Jones' office . . . May I help you?
Pat:	This is Pat Gates. I need to make an appointment.
Secretary:	The next appointment is in December.
Pat:	December? No, I'm sick. I need an appointment fast!
Secretary:	OK. What is the problem?
Pat:	I'm not sure, but I feel tired and sick all the time.
Secretary:	Maybe we can get you in Friday.
Pat:	Yes, Friday is good. What time?
Secretary:	2:30?
Pat:	Thank you, 2:30 is fine.
Secretary:	Good. See you then. Good-bye.
Pat:	Good-bye.

Look at the story and answer the questions.

1. Who is Pat's doctor?

   _____

2. What is Pat's problem?

   _____

3. What day is Pat's appointment?

   _____

4. What time is Pat's appointment?

   _____

Write the words next to the pictures.

nine   five   pine

 1. _____

 2. _____

 3. _____

mice   ice   price

 4. _____

 5. _____

 6. _____

lime   time   dime

 7. _____

 8. _____

 9. _____

bite   bike   wife

 10. _____

 11. _____

12. _____

Write the words next to the pictures.

bone   cone   code

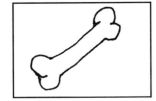

1. _____

2. _____

3. _____

nose   rose   close

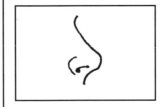

4. _____

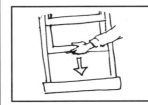

5. _____

6. _____

poke   robe   smoke

7. _____

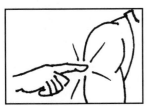

8. _____

9. _____

phone   home   hole

10. _____

11. _____

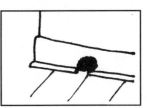

12. _____

Circle the words you hear.

1.	snail	nail	sail
2.	sale	kale	scale
3.	sneak	neat	seat
4.	cool	school	tool
5.	shirt	skirt	dirt
6.	nap	sap	snap
7.	kin	sin	skin
8.	snake	make	sake

Listen to the teacher. Write the words.

1. _____   5. _____

2. _____   6. _____

3. _____   7. _____

4. _____   8. _____

Pat Goes to the Doctor

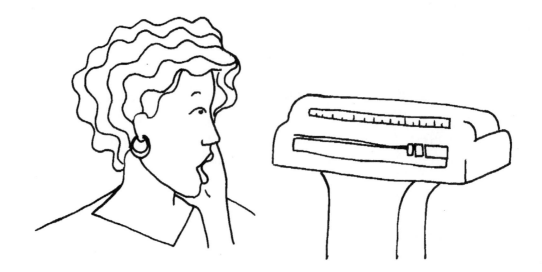

 1. Pat is sad.

2. Sam pokes Pat and says, "Come on."

3. "I will drive you to the clinic at 2:30."

4. "I'm sure Dr. Jones can help."

5. Pat says, "I hope so."

6. "I need a cure fast."

7. "I'm sick all the time, and it's not fun."

8. Pat gets on the scale. 150 pounds!

9. 150 pounds is too much!

10. Dr. Jones checks Pat.

11. Pat has lab tests too.

12. Pat is fine.

13. Dr. Jones tells Pat, "You don't need a cure."

14. "You are having a baby."

15. "The baby is due in June!"

Circle the letters of the correct answers.

1. Where is Pat's appointment?

   a. at the clinic

   b. at the school

   c. at work

2. How is Pat?

   a. happy

   b. OK

   c. sad

3. Who checks Pat?

   a. Sam

   b. Buddy

   c. Dr. Jones

4. What time is the appointment?

   a. 2:00

   b. 2:30

   c. 3:30

5. When is the baby due?

   a. in July

   b. in June

   c. in January

Circle the word for each picture.

   1. tub   tube

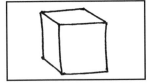   2. cub   cube

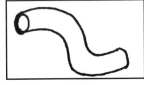   3. tub   tube

   4. cut   cute

   5. hop   hope

   6. rob   robe

   7. rob   robe

   8. not   note

16 The Baby

1. The baby will come in June.

2. Things will not stay the same.

3. Pat hopes Sam is happy about the baby.

4. Sam hopes Pat is glad too.

5. Will they have a boy or a girl? Will they have twins?

6. Will the baby have Pat's nose?

7. Will the baby have Sam's smile?

8. Can Pat still work? How much is day care?

9. Will Sam need 2 jobs?

10. Will Sam have time to spend with his family?

11. Maybe they will have problems.

12. But they are very excited about the baby.

What do you think? Answer the questions.

1. Can Pat still work?

   _____

2. Will Sam need 2 jobs?

   _____

3. Is day care expensive?

   _____

4. Will Sam have time to spend with his family?

   _____

5. Will they have problems?

   _____

Read. Cover, listen, and write the words again.

1. June   1. _____

2. same   2. _____

3. hope   3. _____

4. time   4. _____

5. nose   5. _____

6. stay   6. _____

7. smile   7. _____

8. spend   8. _____

 A Baby Has to Have a Lot of Things

🎧 1. Pat will have a baby in the spring.

2. Sam is happy. Pat is happy too.

3. But a baby has to have a lot of things.

4. A baby is expensive.

5. Sam and Pat go to the mall.

6. They get cash at the bank.

7. They go to Baby Land.

8. Baby Land is a big shop.

9. Pat says, "We have $75."

10. "We have to think."

11. "That swing is beautiful, but it costs too much."

12. "We need to get a crib."

13. "We need a crib, not a swing."

14. Sam and Pat see a crib.

15. It has a big pink mattress.

16. It has a soft pink blanket.

17. The baby will sleep well in this crib.

18. It is beautiful, but too expensive.

19. It is $150.

20. The next crib is OK, but it is not beautiful.

21. It has a good mattress.

22. It has no blanket.

23. It is $100.

24. The last crib is not good.

25. It is junk. But it is cheap.

26. It is only $50.

27. Sam and Pat are sad.

28. They cannot get a crib.

Write Yes or No.   **Yes or No**

1. Sam and Pat go to a baby shop.   _____

2. Pat will have a baby in the fall.   _____

3. They get milk at the bank.   _____

4. They go to Baby Land.   _____

5. They have $200.   _____

6. They get a swing.   _____

7. They get a crib.   _____

8. They are happy!   _____

Fill in the blanks with the correct words.

swing   think   things   spring   bank   pink

1. Pat will have a baby in the _____.

2. "We need a crib, not a _____."

3. The crib has a _____ blanket.

4. "We have to _____."

5. They get cash at the _____.

6. A baby has to have a lot of _____.

Circle the words you hear.

1. sink   sing

2. king   wink

3. sting   skunk

4. long   lung

5. think   thing

6. swing   tank

7. ring   sink

8. lung   drink

We Have No Crib

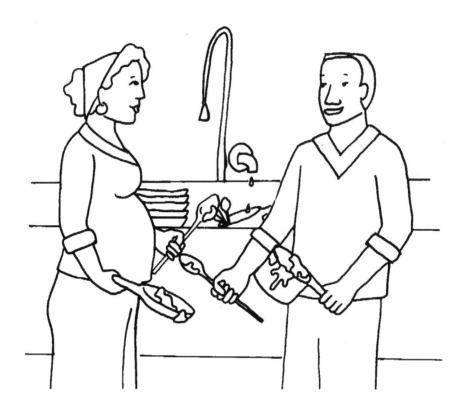

1. Pat is at school.

2. She is at work.

3. She and Hank are at the sink.

4. "How are you?" says Hank.

5. "How's the baby?"

6. "I am fine. The baby is fine."

7. "But we have no crib for the baby."

8. Hank says, "No problem."

9. "My children are big."

10. "I have a crib."

11. "It is old, but it is still good."

12. "How much?" says Pat.

13. "You can have it for free."

14. "I am happy to give it to you."

15. "Thank you, Hank."

16. "You are a good friend and a big help!"

Write Yes or No.   *Yes* or *No*

1. Pat works at the market.   _____

2. She and Hank are at the sink.   _____

3. Hank has an old crib.   _____

4. Hank has a bad crib.   _____

5. Pat gets the crib for $1.   _____

6. Pat gets the crib for free.   _____

7. Hank is sad to give it to her.   _____

8. Pat says, "Thank you, Hank."   _____

Listen. Finish the words with *ink*, *ank*, or *ing*.
Copy the words.

1. s_____   _____

2. spr_____   _____

3. th_____   _____

4. st_____   _____

5. th_____   _____

6. b_____   _____

7. p_____   _____

8. sw_____   _____

Not a Good Spot

 1. Sam and Pat go to the Shop Well Market.

2. It is seven o'clock.

3. The traffic is bad.

4. Sam has to find a spot for the van.

5. He cannot find a spot.

6. Pat says, "It will not take long."

7. "I can get a gallon of milk and a muffin for me."

8. Pat is in the market.

9. Sam is in the van.

10. Then he sees a spot for the van.

11. But the spot is next to the exit.

12. It is not a good spot.

13. Sam says, "That's OK."

Write Yes or No.

1. Sam gets a good spot. _____

2. They are at the beach. _____

3. It is seven o'clock. _____

4. Sam has to find a spot. _____

5. The traffic is bad. _____

6. Sam is in the market. _____

7. Pat is in the market. _____

8. The spot is next to the exit. _____

Fill in the blanks with the correct words.

exit   cannot   traffic   gallon   seven   market

1. The _____ is bad.

2. It is _____ o'clock.

3. He _____ find a spot.

4. Pat is in the _____.

5. The spot is next to the _____.

6. "I can get a _____ of milk.

20 The Ticket

 1. Pat has a big bag.

2. She has a gallon of milk, a dozen eggs, and a muffin.

3. "I can take that," says Sam.

4. Sam says, "You are pregnant."

5. "You cannot pick up too much."

6. Sam and Pat pay.

7. They go to the van.

8. A red ticket is on the van.

9. Sam is upset.

10. "A ticket!" yells Sam.

11. "A ticket is expensive!"

12. Sam has the ticket.

13. He has the ticket in his pocket.

14. "Tomorrow," says Sam.

15. "I will pay the ticket tomorrow."

Write _Yes_ or _No_.   **_Yes_ or _No_**

1. Pat has a gallon of pop.   _____

2. A red ticket is on the van.   _____

3. Sam is happy.   _____

4. A ticket is not expensive.   _____

5. He has the ticket in his bag.   _____

6. "I will pay next week," says Sam.   _____

7. Sam is upset.   _____

Fill in the blanks with the correct words.

cannot   pregnant   pocket   ticket   upset

1. Sam says, "You are _____ .

2. "You _____ pick up too much."

3. A red _____ is on the van.

4. Sam is _____.

5. He has the ticket in his _____ .

Make a line under each syllable. Read each word.

1. cannot

2. traffic

3. happen

4. muffin

5. gallon

6. mitten

7. cotton

8. Boston

9. upset

10. dentist

11. pocket

12. jacket

13. bathtub

14. exit

15. finish

16. seven

17. polish

18. habit

Match the syllables.

Write the words again.

1. cot   fic

   gal   ton

   traf   lon

1. _____

  _____

  _____

2. bath   et

   jack   set

   up   tub

2. _____

  _____

  _____

3. fin   it

   ex   en

   sev   ish

3. _____

  _____

  _____

Lesson

The Contest

 1. Buddy is at school.

2. At 10:00, the bell rings.

3. Buddy has to run.

4. He has a trumpet lesson.

5. Buddy is in the hall.

6. He sees an ad.

7. The ad says, "Big Trumpet Contest!"

8. "Win cash!"

9. "$100 for the best song!"

10. Buddy thinks he can win.

11. He will ask Mr. Willis to help.

12. Mr. Willis is the teacher.

13. The contest is in six weeks.

14. Buddy and Mr. Willis work hard.

15. They play every day.

16. The first lesson is not good.

17. Buddy does not play well.

18. Mr. Willis says, "You can do it. Come on!"

19. Buddy does not rest.

20. He plays at school.

21. He plays at home.

22. The second lesson is good.

23. He thinks he can win . . . maybe!?

Write *Yes* or *No*.   **Yes or No**

1. Buddy has a math lesson.   _____

2. He is at school.   _____

3. He sees an ad.   _____

4. The ad says, "Win cash!"   _____

5. The contest is next week.   _____

6. Buddy plays a drum.   _____

7. Buddy rests.   _____

8. He plays at home.   _____

Fill in the blanks with the correct words.

lesson   Contest   rest   second   best

1. The ad says, "Big Trumpet _____ .

2. The first _____ is not good.

3. The _____ lesson is good.

4. Buddy does not _____ .

5. "$100 for the _____ song."

22 Second Best

 1. It is the big day.

2. Today is the contest.

3. Pat and Granddad come.

4. Sam cannot come.

5. He has to work.

6. Seven hundred kids will listen.

7. Buddy has to play last.

8. He plays a long, sad song.

9. Then Granddad and Pat jump up.

10. They yell and clap.

11. All the children clap too.

12. But Buddy does not win.

13. He is not the best.

14. He is second.

15. He gets a red ribbon.

16. And he gets a check.

17. Buddy is not upset.

18. He is glad.

19. He has a ribbon and a check.

Write Yes or No.

1. Pat and Sam come.   _____

2. Sam cannot come.   _____

3. Sam has to work.   _____

4. Granddad and Pat jump up.   _____

5. They yell and clap.   _____

6. Buddy is second.   _____

7. Buddy is the best.   _____

8. Buddy has a ribbon and a check.   _____

Fill in the blanks with the correct words.

cannot   hundred   song   ribbon   upset

1. Seven _____ kids will listen.

2. He plays a long, sad _____ .

3. He gets a red _____ .

4. Sam _____ come.

5. Buddy is not _____ .

Underline the syllables and then write the syllables.

1. children _____ _____

2. contest _____ _____

3. second _____ _____

4. lesson _____ _____

5. hundred _____ _____

6. ribbon _____ _____

7. upset _____ _____

8. cannot _____ _____

9. pocket _____ _____

 1. Sam and Pat are in bed.

2. Sam drinks hot milk.

3. Pat and Sam listen to the rain.

4. Then, Pat has a pain.

5. "We have to go," says Pat.

6. "We have to go now."

7. Pat has her bag.

8. Sam is a mess.

9. At last they go to the van.

10. At the clinic Sam is in the hall.

11. Pat is with the doctor.

12. Sam cannot think.

13. Sam cannot sit.

14. He cannot read.

15. The doctor comes at last.

16. He says, "It's a girl!"

Write *Yes* or *No*.   **Yes or No**

1. Sam drinks tea.   _____

2. Sam and Pat are at work.   _____

3. Pat has her bag.   _____

4. Sam is a mess.   _____

5. Pat and Sam go to the clinic.   _____

6. Pat is with the doctor.   _____

7. Sam is in the hall.   _____

8. The doctor says, "It's a boy!"   _____

Listen to the teacher. Fill in the blanks with one of the following:

ank   ang   ink   ank   ing

1. r_____

2. r_____

3. th_____

4. th_____

5. h_____

6. s_____

7. s_____

8. w_____

9. dr_____

10. st_____

24 The Baby Is Well

 1. The baby is well.

2. Pat is well too.

3. She is very happy.

4. The baby is pink and small.

5. Buddy and Granddad come.

6. They come in the taxi with Gus.

7. They all come to see the baby.

8. Bess is her name.

9. Sam picks up Bess.

10. Then Buddy picks up Bess.

11. Granddad and Gus smile.

12. They are all content to have Bess in the family.

Write *Yes* or *No*.   ***Yes* or *No***

1. The baby is pink and small.   _____

2. They are all sad.   _____

3. Buddy and Granddad cannot come.   _____

4. Sam picks up Bess.   _____

5. Bess is her name.   _____

6. Granddad and Gus smile.   _____

7. They all come to see the baby.   _____

8. They are all content.   _____

Write seven words that end with *ll*, *ss*, or *ff*.

1. _____

2. _____

3. _____

4. _____

5. _____

6. _____

7. _____

Phonetic Word Grids

Phonetic Word Grid 1

Name: _____

bee   peel   sheep   sweep   three

meet   feet   beet   tree   sleep

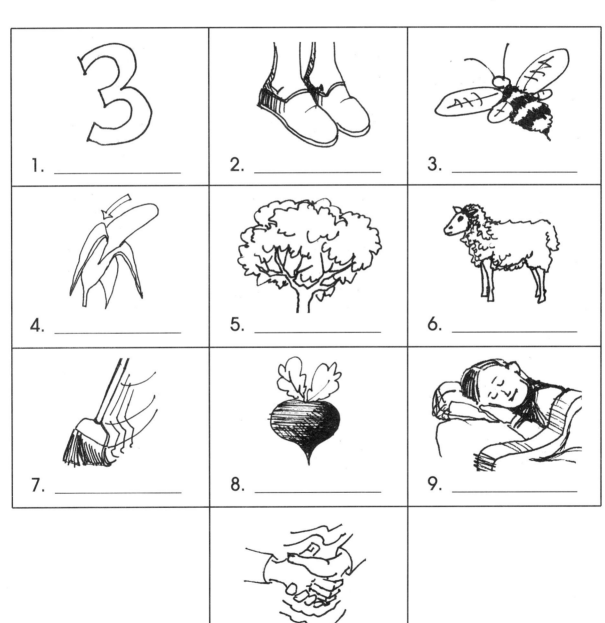

1. _____

2. _____

3. _____

4. _____

5. _____

6. _____

7. _____

8. _____

9. _____

10. _____

Phonetic Word Grid 2

Name: _____

peach   beach   eat   seat   meat

lean   bean   heat   clean   ear

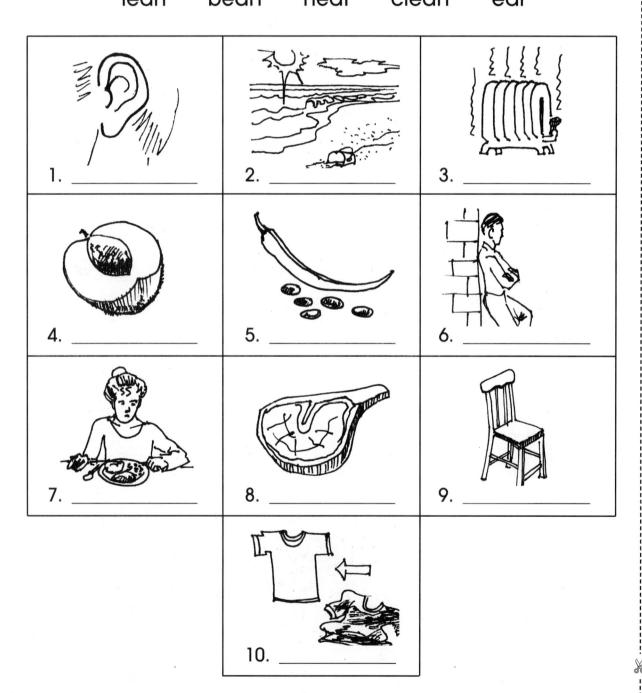

1. _____

2. _____

3. _____

4. _____

5. _____

6. _____

7. _____

8. _____

9. _____

10. _____

Phonetic Word Grid 3

Name: _____

train   pail   jail   sail   nail   snail

rain   chain   mail   wait   paint   pain

1. _____	2. _____	3. _____
4. _____	5. _____	6. _____
7. _____	8. _____	9. _____
10. _____	11. _____	12. _____

Phonetic Word Grid 4

Name: _____

May   say   pray   lay

pay   day   way   play

1. _____

2. _____

3. _____

4. _____

5. _____

6. _____

7. _____

8. _____

Phonetic Word Grid 5

Name: _____

frog   grill   grass   pray   press

friend   free   grab   present   grin

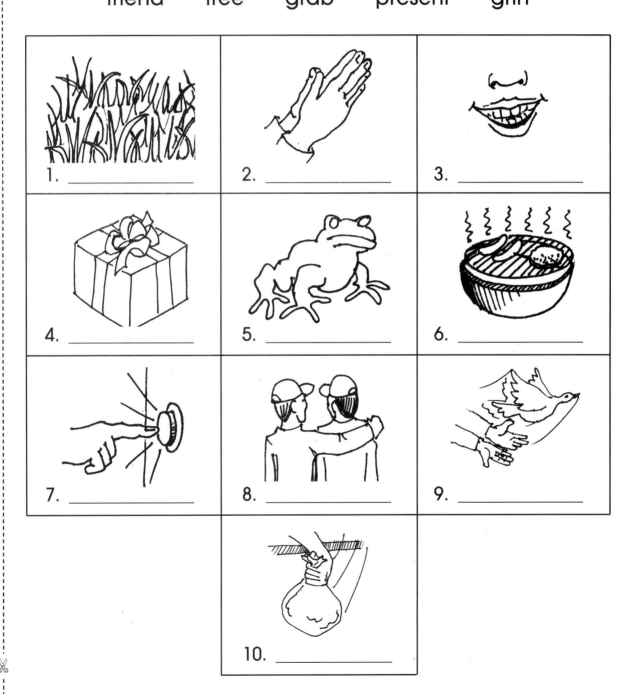

1. _____

2. _____

3. _____

4. _____

5. _____

6. _____

7. _____

8. _____

9. _____

10. _____

Phonetic Word Grid 6

Name: _____

glass   flag   plug   glove   plate

plane   flex   plant   flip

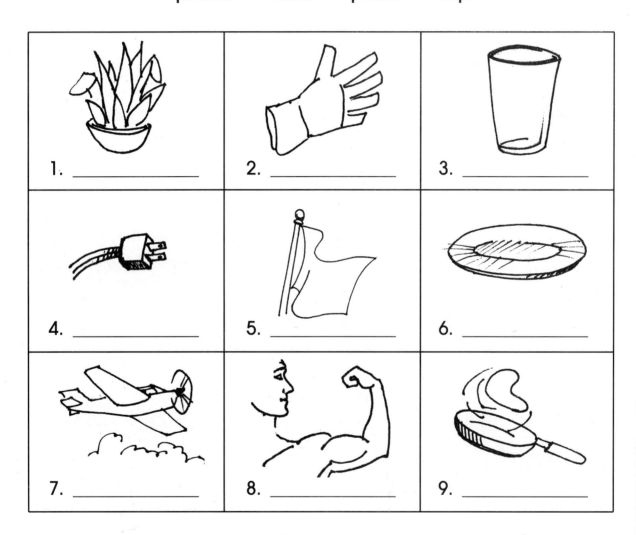

1. _____   2. _____   3. _____

4. _____   5. _____   6. _____

7. _____   8. _____   9. _____

Phonetic Word Grid 7

Name: _____

grab   brick   grass   brush   grin

grade   bridge   grape   braid   grill

1. _____

2. _____

3. _____

4. _____

5. _____

6. _____

7. _____

8. _____

9. _____

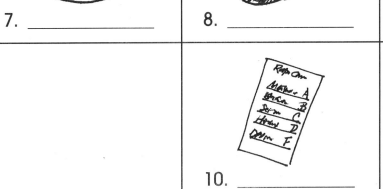

10. _____

Phonetic Word Grid 8

Name: _____

cake   grades   plate   snake   plane

shave   cane   wave   cape   tape

1. _____

2. _____

3. _____

4. _____

5. _____

6. _____

7. _____

8. _____

9. _____

10. _____

Phonetic Word Grid 9

Name: _____

write   dime   bite   bike   nine   drive

mice   ice   five   rice   pine   smile

1. _____	2. _____	3. _____
4. _____	5. _____	6. _____
7. _____	8. _____	9. _____
10. _____	11. _____	12. _____

Phonetic Word Grid 10

Name: _____

swim   switch   twelve   twenty

twin   sweep   swing

1. _____

2. _____

3. _____

4. _____

5. _____

6. _____

7. _____

Phonetic Word Grid 11

Name: _____

smoke   rope   nose   bone   rose

stove   note   robe   cone   phone

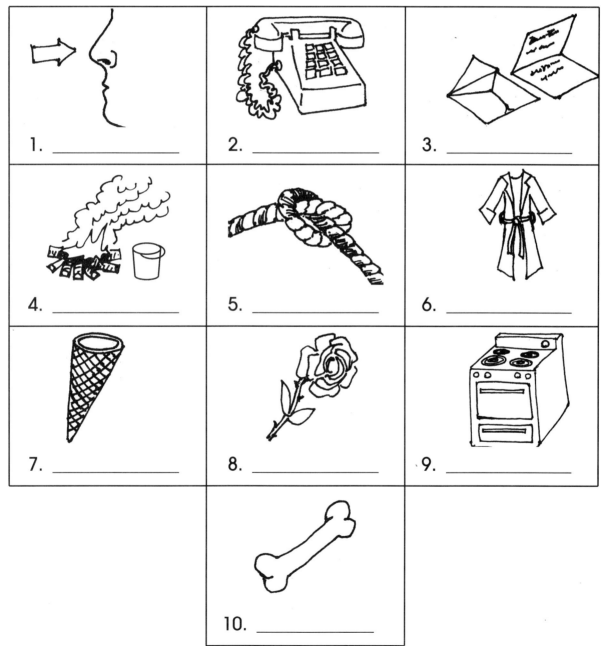

1. _____

2. _____

3. _____

4. _____

5. _____

6. _____

7. _____

8. _____

9. _____

10. _____

Phonetic Word Grid 12

Name: _____

snail   scale   skate   sneeze   skirt

school   skull   snake   scarf   skunk

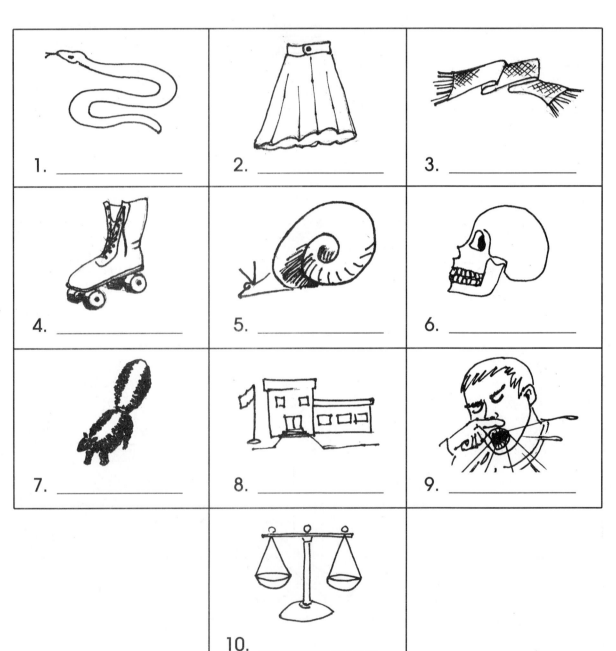

1. _____

2. _____

3. _____

4. _____

5. _____

6. _____

7. _____

8. _____

9. _____

10. _____

Key Word Cards for Phonics

short vowels				consonants			
front		**back**		**front**		**back**	
o		o	/o/	f		f	/f/
e		e	/e/	h		h	/h/
a		a	/a/	l		l	/l/
u		u	/u/	m		m	/m/
i		i	/i/	n		n	/n/

Key Word Cards for Phonics

consonants

front	back		front	back	
r	r	/r/	c	c	/c/
s	s	/s/	d	d	/d/
v	v	/v/	g	g	/g/
z	z	/z/	j	j	/j/
b	b	/b/	k	k	/k/

Key Word Cards for Phonics

consonants

front	back
p	p /p/
qu	qu /qu/
t	t /t/
w	w /w/
y	y /y/
x	x /x/

consonant digraphs

front	back
th	th /th/
sh	sh /sh/
ch	ch /ch/

Suggested Listening Scripts

Listening activities are indicated by this icon: 💬. The teacher can either use the **Suggested Listening Scripts** that are found here, or choose appropriate words that go with the lesson for dictation. These words should reinforce the phonetic element of the lesson. In addition, the **Phonetic Word Grids** can be assigned for supplemental practice as each new sound is introduced. They are listed in the **Lesson Chart** at the beginning of the book.

Page 27 Write.

Have students cover the words while you dictate them.

Page 29 Write.

1. crab
2. trash
3. crack
4. tree
5. crib

Page 42 Listen and write the words.

1. cake
2. take
3. make
4. wake
5. hate
6. late
7. date
8. state

Page 47 Write.

1. glass
2. glad
3. bleed
4. blame
5. blade
6. bless
7. black

Page 63 Listen to the teacher and write the words again.

1. face
2. space
3. race
4. rice
5. mice
6. ice

Page 64 Circle the words you hear.

1. rice
2. space
3. lake
4. bike
5. make

Page 64 Listen and write.

1. make
2. bake
3. bike
4. like
5. lake

Page 76 Listen to the teacher. Write s or sl under the pictures.

1. six
2. sled
3. slip
4. sun
5. slam
6. sit
7. slim
8. sick
9. Sam
10. sad

Page 81 Circle the words you hear.

1. nail
2. sale
3. sneak
4. tool
5. shirt
6. snap
7. skin
8. snake

Page 81 Listen to the teacher. Write the words.

1. nail
2. neat
3. skirt
4. shirt
5. snap
6. sap
7. skin
8. kin

Page 89 Read. Cover, listen, and write the words again.

Have students cover the words while you dictate them.

Page 95 Circle the words you hear.

1. sink
2. wink
3. sting
4. long
5. think
6. swing
7. ring
8. drink

Page 99 Listen. Finish the words with *ink*, *ank*, or *ing* and copy the words.

1. sink
2. spring
3. thank
4. stink
5. thing
6. bank
7. pink
8. swing

Page 124 Listen to the teacher. Fill in the blanks with one of the following:

1. ring
2. rink
3. thank
4. thing
5. hang
6. sank
7. sing
8. wing
9. drink
10. sting